Children of the Old Testament

AN ARCH BOOK ANTHOLOGY

CHILDREN OF THE OLD TESTAMENT: An Arch Book Anthology

From
ADAM'S STORY   Concordia Publishing House © 1985
THE BOY WHO SAVED HIS FAMILY   Concordia Publishing House © 1966
GOD'S GIFT BABY   Concordia Publishing House © 1976
THE BOY WITH A SLING   Concordia Publishing House © 1965
GOOD LITTLE KING JOSIAH   Concordia Publishing House © 1978

Library of Congress Cataloging-in-Publication Data

Main entry under title:

    Children of the Old Testament.

    Contents: Adam's story / by Louis Ulmer—The boy who saved his family
/ by Alyce Bergey—God's gift baby / by LaVonne Neff—[etc.]
    1. Children in the Bible—Biography—Juvenile literature. 2. Bible.
O.T.—Biography—Juvenile literature. [1. Children in the Bible. 2. Bible.
O.T.—Biography]
BS576.C46 1986   221.9'505 [920]   85-17129
ISBN 0-570-06207-1

1 2 3 4 5 6 7 8 9 10 PP 95 94 93 92 91 90 89 88 87 86

Adam's
Story

Genesis 1 and 2:18-22 for Children

Written by Louise Ulmer
Illustrated by Kathy Mitter

ARCH BOOKS

Copyright © 1985 CONCORDIA PUBLISHING HOUSE

3558 S. Jefferson Avenue, St. Louis, MO 63118

Manufactured in the United States of America

Two little boys named Abel and Cain
Lay on a hill making flower chains.
"Where did we come from?" Abel asked Cain.
"Let's ask Father if he can explain."

They walked through the meadow and stopped at a pond.
They fed little rabbits and petted a fawn.
"Where did you come from?" Cain asked a doe.
There was so much Abel wanted to know.

Supper was ready when the boys found Eve
Making a salad out of fresh green leaves.
Adam came home from his hard day's work
Planting his garden in the rich, brown dirt.

After the dinner, in the campfire's glow,
The boys asked their father all they wanted to know.
"Sit on my lap," said the father to his sons.
"I'll tell you how the heavens and the earth were begun."

"Once at the dawning of a brand new world,
God made the universe and gave it a twirl.
He looked at the darkness that blackened the night,
Then scattered the stillness with *Let there be light!'*

"Light burst the darkness and scattered it away.
Dazzling brightness sent shimmering rays.
The light and the dark went separate ways—
Evening and morning were the very first day.

"On the second bright morning, He created the sky,
But only the Lord knows how and why.
No bird or invention that's able to fly
Could reach to the end of God's heaven so high.

"On the third bright morning, God looked around.
'I'll separate the water from the high, dry ground.
The water on the globe I shall call great seas.
I'll color up the landscape with grass and trees.'

"He raised all the mountains with His wonderful powers.
He sparkled up the earth with dewy, fresh flowers.
Waterfalls rippled into glassy blue pools.
Everything in nature was refreshing and cool.

"On the fourth bright morning, He liked what He'd done.
He rolled up a fireball and called it the sun.
A moon He arranged to give silvery light,
And billions of stars that twinkle at night.

"On the fifth bright morning, He worked on the birds,
Creatures that fly and sing without words.
The eagle mounted up at God's command.
By the wisdom of God hawks flew overland.

"He gave to the peacocks fabulous tails
And little topknots to the cute brown quails.
He made all the lady birds and flashy, bright males.
He gave the sweetest song to the nightingales.

"For the rest of the day He made something new.
He invented all the fish and marine life, too.
He filled up the oceans and the riverbeds deep
With fish that swim and creatures that creep.

"The pretty, shiny goldfish and the monstrous whales
Leaped in the water and splashed their tails.
Clams on the ocean floor started making pearls.
The octopi and sea horses stretched their ends in curls.

"On the sixth bright morning He had much to do,
Forming all the reptiles and the animals, too,
So He turned His attention to the beasts on the land—
Zebras in the meadows and fleas in the sand.

"Fireflies and dragonflies with tails of blue,
Insects and butterflies with wings that flew.
From the crocodile in swampland to the little brown shrew.
God formed them all to the last kangaroo.

"Monkeys in the jungle and koalas in the trees,
Pandas in the bamboo, and hives of bees,
Leopards with their furry coats, seals upon the ice,
God liked them all and said, 'How nice!'

"When animals were finished, God created a man,
A two-legged body with thumbs on his hands.
God made him smarter than the creatures but lo:
Man was the only one whom God gave a soul.

"He called the man Adam, and said 'This do:
Name all My animals, two by two.'
So I named all the animals and when I was through,
God said, 'I'll make a helper just for you.'

"A man needs a person to share his life.
So God made me a beautiful wife.
'Live and love together,' said God to us two,
'And take care of everything I've given to you.'

"On the seventh bright morning, God stopped to rest.
'I'll honor this day and keep it for the best.
My people need a rest from the work they do.
I'll make this a holiday, and they should too.' "

Cain was asleep when the story was through.
Eve put the boys to bed, then she slept, too.
Adam prayed to God, then put out the light,
And the evening and the morning made another good night.

DEAR PARENTS:

The writer of the New Testament Letter to the Hebrews states the truth explicitly: "Every house is builded by some man, but the Builder of all things is God" (3:4). Of all men since the beginning of time, none most likely has been more aware of this than Adam, who was created in the image of God by God Himself, who "in the cool of the day" shared with his Creator the joys of a perfect world, and who, with Eve, experienced firsthand the profound impact and tragedy of the Fall, not only on himself and Eve, but on all of God's creation as well.

We can only imagine the stories of paradise that Adam probably told his young sons, Cain and Abel. Yet there was always one more story for Adam to tell, too: how through his own disobedience sin and death entered into God's world. And how even in this most flagrant rejection of God's love and care, God reached out in love to His children and provided for them a ransom from the eternal death that was their—and our—just fate. That Ransom was His own Son, Jesus.

Tell your own children of God's love and care for them. Pray for them and with them frequently. And let God's love for you and for all His children be reflected in your love for those God has placed in your care.

THE EDITOR

THE BOY WHO SAVED HIS FAMILY

GENESIS 37–50 FOR CHILDREN

Written by Alyce Bergey
Illustrated by Betty Wind

ARCH Books

© 1966 CONCORDIA PUBLISHING HOUSE, ST. LOUIS, MISSOURI

Once there was a boy named Joseph.
He was one of thirteen children.
Their father was Jacob.
Their family had lived in the land of Canaan
ever since their great-grandfather Abraham.

Jacob owned many animals.
His children took care of the sheep and goats.

Jacob loved Joseph best of all his sons.
He gave him a long coat with long sleeves;
this showed that Joseph was to be the leader.
The boy was very proud of his coat.

His brothers could see that their father
loved Joseph more than any of them.
They hated Joseph because of this.

Once Joseph told his brothers:
"I dreamed we were tying
bundles of wheat.
Your bundles bowed down to mine.
This made the brothers angry.

Another time Joseph told them,
"I dreamed that the sun and moon
and eleven stars bowed down to me."
"Do you think we will bow down
to you?" the brothers laughed.

One day Joseph was looking for his brothers.
"Let's kill the dreamer," they said
when they saw him coming.
"No," said the oldest brother.
"Let's put him in this deep hole."

So they took away
his new coat
and put
him in
the deep
hole.

Just then some men rode by.
"Would you like to buy a boy?"
the brothers called out.
"You could sell him in Egypt."
"Yes, we will buy him," said the men.

The brothers put goat's blood
on Joseph's coat.
When Jacob saw the coat, he cried,
"A wild beast has killed my boy."
He was very sad.

On his way to
Egypt Joseph cried,
"Will I ever see Father again?
Why did my brothers do this to me?"

Then Joseph thought:
"God can make bad things
turn out good." Joseph wasn't so
afraid anymore.

In Egypt Joseph was
sold to a rich man.
He had to work without pay.
But his master liked his work,
and God was with him.

ne night the king of Egypt
nt for all his wise men.
e said: "I dreamed that I saw
ven fat cows and seven thin cows.
he thin cows ate up the fat ones.

Then I saw seven good ears of wheat
nd seven bad ears of wheat.
he bad ears ate up the good ones.
'hat does this mean?"
ut none of the wise men knew.

Then one of his servants said,
"Joseph knows the meaning of dreams."
The king sent for him at once.
Joseph was a grown man now.

Joseph explained the dreams:
"O king, for seven years
much food will grow,
and for seven years nothing will.
Store up food in the good years.
Then there will be food
for the bad years."

"You are very wise,"
the king told Joseph.
"Take care of things
for me."

The king gave Joseph
new clothes,
and the king's ring
and carriage.

Soon the seven good years came.
Everything grew so that Joseph
had to have new barns built
to store the wheat.

Then came the bad years.
But people could buy food
from Joseph.

So Joseph's big brothers came, too.
They bowed way down before him.
They did not know he was Joseph.
But he knew them.

"You are spies!" he said.
"Oh, no, sir!" they cried.
"We have come only to buy food
for our family."

"No, you are spies," Joseph said.
"Put them in jail!" he ordered.

After three days the brothers
were taken back to Joseph.
"Now we are paying for what we did
to Joseph," they whispered, afraid.

Joseph heard
what they said.
He felt sorry
for them.

"I am Joseph, your brother!" he cried.
"I am not angry with you anymore.
God brought me to Egypt
to save us all from hunger."

The brothers
were so happy!
They had long
been sorry for
what they had
done to Joseph.

They went to get
the whole family.

How happy Jacob was!
"Lord," he cried, "You are taking
such good care of us."

God said: "I shall go with you to Egypt.
Someday I will bring your family back
and give them this land."

Jacob and his children moved to Egypt.
Joseph cried for joy when he saw his father.

The family got sacks of flour,
and good grass land for their animals.
And God was with them.
But one day they would return home.

Dear Parents:

The story of Joseph is not just an adventure tale, standing all by itself. It is a story about how God can change even the worst things into something good and wonderful in His own good time. It forms a part of the great adventure of the people of God, Israel, and of God's saving plan for mankind.

God had brought Joseph's great-grandfather Abraham into the land of Canaan, there to bring up a new people who would differ from all the surrounding nations by their faith in Him. Nothing could block God's saving plan; not even such disasters as famine or the actions of Abraham's great-grandchildren could. Sold into slavery by his brothers, Joseph became God's instrument in the saving of Egypt and his own people from hunger. The family tragedy became their salvation, and eventually ours because it was from Abraham's family that the Savior of all nations was to be born.

Can you help your child see the deeper meaning of the Joseph story and recall it in times of fear and anxiety? And will you help him grow not only in knowing the various Bible stories but also in understanding how they belong to one great plan of God?

THE EDITOR

GOD'S GIFT BABY

1 Samuel 1—2 FOR CHILDREN

Written by LaVonne Neff
Illustrated by Don Kueker

ARCH Books
Copyright © 1976 CONCORDIA PUBLISHING HOUSE, ST. LOUIS, MISSOURI
MANUFACTURED IN THE UNITED STATES OF AMERICA
ALL RIGHTS RESERVED
ISBN 0-570-06113-X

In Egypt the Israelites
Forgot their God.
They were forced to obey evil men.
So God led them out
To a promised new land,
Where they promptly forgot Him again.

God looked at His people,
And what did He see?
Drunken priests taking naps in the street,
Rich robbers in search
Of more money to steal,
Cruel husbands, of more wives to beat.

The old high priest Eli,
God's ruler on earth,
Sat and pondered and grew tired and grey,
While in front of the people
His sons broke God's Law
In every conceivable way.

"I must speak to My people,"
God said; "I must warn
Them to listen to My words again."
But all of the servants
That God had ordained,
If not wicked, were tired old men.

6

In the midst of the gloom
And the godless decay
Lived Elkanah, and Hannah his wife.

They loved God and each other,
But Hannah was sad—
No child came to brighten her life.

Elkanah went up
To the temple each year
To give offerings, to feast, and to pray.
And every year Hannah
Would stand in the court
Of the women, and to herself say,

"This year I'm alone,
But I do love my God,
And I come in His presence with joy.
Perhaps by next year
He will grant me my wish
And will send me my own baby boy."

Each year, like the last,
Hannah fervently prayed,
And grew older, and multiplied fears

That she'd die with no children,
A woman despised—
Until one day she let loose the tears

That she'd locked in her heart,
And she fell to the ground,
Where she wailed and sobbed out her woe.
She didn't know Eli
Was watching her pray.
She was startled to hear him say, "Go

And clean yourself up,
Woman. We have enough
To do around here without you
Drunken women, who ought
To be home with your kids!"
"Oh, sir," cried out Hannah, "I, too,

Am a lover of God,
And I'm not at all drunk.
But, Priest Eli, my soul is on fire!
One thing I ask God for,
One thing I must have,
And God has withheld my desire."

Kind Eli, now seeing
The tears on her cheeks,
The worry lines deep in her face,
Said, "May the Lord give you
Whatever you want.
May He make you rejoice in His grace."

Elkanah and Hannah
Went home, full of peace.
No longer was Hannah forlorn.
She sang lullabies
And collected small clothes
And prepared for her son to be born.

In less than a year
After Hannah's sad prayer,
Elkanah had something to tell:
"A son has been born
To my Hannah and me!
He's God's gift, and his name's Samuel."

"God's gift!" whispered Hannah.
Her heart filled with joy.
"But Samuel isn't my own.
I can't do with him
Whatever I please.
This baby is really God's loan."

Elkanah went up
To the temple that year,
And the next, and the next; but his wife
Stayed at home with her baby.
"I've just a few years
To get Samuel ready for life,"

Hannah said to her husband.
But in the fourth year,
When young Samuel had just turned three,
Hannah said, "It is time
For my gift-son to go
Serve the Giver who gave him to me."

"This is my son,"
Hannah said to Eli.
"God lent him to me for three years.
Now I give him to you,
To the temple, to God—"
Hannah struggled to keep back her tears.

"I will see you again.
I will make all your clothes.
I will visit you yearly, at least.

Just remember, my boy
(If you can, so can I),
You're not mine, you are
God's little priest!"

And God smiled at those three,
Mother, son, and old man.
"Here," he said, "is the one who will tell
All my wandering children
To come home again—
Little prophet, the boy Samuel!"

DEAR PARENTS:

The history of God's relationship with His people is one-sided. The Israelites regularly betray God; God regularly sends a spiritual savior to bring them back. Each of God's great servants—Moses and Samuel predominant among them—was a kind of forerunner of Christ, the great Savior of us all.

As this story opens, the Children of Israel are once again serving their own selfish interests. Hannah, a childless woman, also seems to be praying selfishly for her own good. But when her prayer is answered, we discover that she regards herself only as a caretaker for the Lord's child. Samuel belongs to God, and after three years Hannah gives her dearly loved child back to God. What a striking contrast to the utter selfishness around her.

Samuel was truly a gift child—a gift to Hannah, his mother; a gift from Hannah to the church; and especially God's gift to His erring children.

We, too, need to remind ourselves that our children really belong to God. We are God's caretakers and have been given a great responsibility. Just consider how Eli, the old priest, cared for God's gift children to him.

Remind your children of their real Father. (In a way you are their earthly sponsors.) Point out to them how they are God's gifts to you. Teach them to love their heavenly Father. Show them how, as in this story, God's gift of love must be shared if it is to grow.

THE EDITOR

The Boy
with
a SLING

1 SAMUEL 16:1—18:5 FOR CHILDREN

Written by
Mary Warren

Illustrated by
Sally Mathews

Long before
Mary or Joseph or Jesus were born,
God said to Samuel, His priest,
"Put oil in your horn,
and go now and find
the Bethlehem boy I have in mind
to be king of my people some day."

ARCH Books

© 1965 CONCORDIA PUBLISHING HOUSE, ST. LOUIS, MISSOURI

LIBRARY OF CONGRESS CATALOG CARD NO. 65-15143
MANUFACTURED IN THE UNITED STATES OF AMERICA
ALL RIGHTS RESERVED
ISBN 0-570-06012-5

It was to the home of Jesse
that Samuel went.
After meeting and greeting his sons,
he asked:
"Are there more?"
And so Jesse sent
to the fields for his youngest,
David the shepherd boy,
handsome and strong.

God said to Samuel:
"You are looking for one to be king —
this is he!
Take holy oil, anoint him for Me!"

Nobody knew
except God and His holy man, Samuel,
what this would do.
Alone on the hills, he had to keep
lions and bears from stealing his sheep,
and the Spirit of God gave him such
courage and might
that the wildest of creatures
he dared to fight!

There was at this time a long war.
The Philistine army
and the Israelites, under King Saul,
camped on two mountains.

Each morning a Philistine giant,
Goliath of Gath,
came down in the Valley of Elah to call
"Is any man there
who will fight against me?
I shall chop off his head
and cut up his body like bread
to toss to the beasts
and the birds!

WHO WILL DARE?"

Goliath the giant put fear
in each Israelite heart with his shout.
His brass armor clinked; his long spear
made even the bravest men doubt
that any could fight him and win.

One day the shepherd boy, David, came
with cheese and some bread
for his brothers
who fought in Saul's army.
Like the others, they ran
when Goliath came down.

When David saw this,
he said with a frown:
"Goliath makes fun of our God!
Does no one believe that the Lord
takes care of His armies in need?

I will fight this giant myself!"

King Saul heard of David's brave words.
He sent for the boy and he smiled.
"You are hardly more than a child!
Goliath knows all about war!
What are *you* offering for?"

Said David: "Out in the field
when either a lion or bear
tried to steal my father's young sheep,
my God helped me fight with him there.
I know in this battle God will
shield and deliver me still!"

Saul put his armor on David:
"Here is my coat of mail . . .
my helmet . . . my very own sword.
Go! In the name of the Lord!"

But Saul's armor was heavy; he fell.
"I cannot wear them, O King!
I am used to only a sling!"

With his sling and his shepherd's crook
David stopped to search at the brook
for some stones.
With these in his bag, he went on
to the place where Goliath of Gath
made the Israelites tremble in fear.
"Who is there?" roared Goliath.

His shield bearer stood before him, but he
was still able to see
David the shepherd boy. And with a sneer
and a laugh that was cruel,
Goliath drew near.

"Why do you pick
such a boy for this fight?
Am I but a dog to be chased with a stick?
Come! I will throw all your bones
to the birds of the air
and the beasts of the field!"

David reached for his stones.
"Your spear is sharp and long and strong;
your shield is great and heavy too.
There is one reason that I came.
You mock the Lord and . . . in His name
I have power to conquer you!"

David's hand dipped in his bag.
Before Goliath had time to see
he put a stone in his sling and — WHEE!

It hit the Philistine in the head;

he staggered, then fell forward —

Goliath was DEAD.

David ran with a glorious shout
and took the giant's heavy sword
and cut his head off. Soon the word
spread through the Philistine camp.
The men raced hard to get away
but the Israelites were close behind
and many Philistines died that day.

Triumphantly they marched to bring
the battle news and Goliath's head
to Saul, the waiting king, who said:
"Your strength from God, O David, wins
Israel this victory;
my army needs such bravery!"

From that day on young David stayed
at court with Saul, who knew he'd need
a captain who was strong to lead
his men in other battles too.

This army training helped him grow
to be, in time, God's chosen king —
he who once had been a boy
who killed a giant with a sling!

Dear Parents:

The story of David and Goliath is so loved by all children because here a "big bully," the giant Goliath, gets outsmarted and defeated by the "little guy," David.

In a way this story stands for the entire history of the People of God. God surprises us again and again by the instruments He chooses: the little nation Israel, the timid Moses (Exodus 4:10-16), the young shepherd boy David, the little nobody Mary, the simple fishermen, the unimpressive speaker Paul (1 Corinthians 2:1-5). God gives His Spirit and power to the least likely people and changes the lives of men and of nations through them.

It is really not David or Moses or any of the important figures of the Bible who is the "hero," but God, who saves His People through them, who "resists the proud" and is the Champion of the oppressed. It is He who gives power to the powerless, wisdom to the simple, and opens up new possibilities where men see only a dead end.

Will you help your child understand this as you talk over the story, and lead him to believe it by the way you yourself deal with the pressures and anxieties of life?

THE EDITOR

GOOD LITTLE KING JOSIAH

2 Kings 22—23 2
Chronicles 34—35 FOR CHILDREN

Written by Mervin Marquardt
Illustrated by Herb Halpern Productions

ARCH Books

Copyright © 1978 CONCORDIA PUBLISHING HOUSE, ST. LOUIS, MISSOURI

MANUFACTURED IN THE UNITED STATES OF AMERICA

ALL RIGHTS RESERVED   ISBN 0-570-06118-0

A long time ago Jerusalem
  Was ruled by a wicked king
Who boasted aloud, "I am the best,
  So God doesn't mean a thing!"

He taxed his people way too much
    And wasted the money he had
On parties and golden clothes and crowns—
    Whatever the latest fad.

Within the palace lived a boy,
  Josiah the prince was he.
Although he was only eight, he was
  As good as he could be.

His favorite sport was archery,
   He centered his arrows in;
But always he smiled cheerfully
   Whenever his friends would win.

Josiah the prince was happy to be
  A child without a care.
But while he was still an eight-year-old,
  The king was killed somewhere.

"Now Josiah's the king," the people sang,
"All hail the child king!
Bow down to Josiah's feet and let
The bells of Jerusalem ring!"

"Josiah, the king"—he liked the sound,
But he didn't know how to rule.
His teachers had never said a thing
About that in the palace school.

So good little King Josiah asked
    Hilkiah the priest, his friend,
To teach him about the government
    And how to govern men.

"Josiah, my king," Hilkiah said,
    The very first thing we do
Is pray on our knees and ask the Lord
    To bless this land anew.

"Josiah and I now ask You, Lord,
    A blessing from heaven above:
The wisdom he needs to rule Your land,
    The beauty of all Your love."

Hilkiah then told the palace guards,
"Summon the teachers quick!
Josiah must learn to be a king
And all about politics."

So the palace guards told the messengers
  Who shouted from the balcony,
"All teachers must come to the palace school
  To teach His Majesty!"

From over the land the teachers came
To Josiah the child king
To teach him about the land he ruled
And all about governing.

They taught him to wear a robe and crown,
   To hold his scepter high,
To sit on his throne (which was too big),
   And how to be dignified.

He learned how to wield a sword and shield
  Without hurting himself, of course;
And how to command his generals,
  And how to saddle a horse.

And when he had learned his servants would
    Bring candy by the crate,
Josiah decided he liked his job,
    That being the king was great.

The only part he didn't like
   Was the king of the neighboring land;
The king of Assyria made Josiah
   Follow his every command.

"We'll destroy you, Josiah," Assyria said,
  "Unless you agree to pay
Us half of your taxes, and worship all
  Our idols every day."

Josiah the king asked, "Should I serve
    Assyrian gods and throne?
In history I learned King David ruled
    By serving the Lord alone.

"Would David have let our people pray
    To Assyrian gods of stone?
Or have given our money half away?
    This cannot be condoned!"

So good little King Josiah sent
   His servants with this decree:
"Destroy all the idols and serve the Lord
   In every community.

"And send me your taxes which I will use
  To repair the house of the Lord.
We'll clean it and shine it and fix it up right;
  The best we can afford."

So the carpenters came, the goldsmiths too,
  And the stonecutters in a parade
To make the temple beautiful,
  As good as the day it was made.

While they were cleaning a storage room,
  They found a most ancient book
That seemed it was important enough
  for the king to take a look.

When Josiah the king had read it all,
    His face was both happy and sad.
"I'm happy because you found a book
    Nobody remembered we had.

"The book is the Law of the Lord our God
    And promises us His grace.
But it also threatens punishment
    If idols we embrace.

"No wonder we served Assyria,
    That was our punishment.
But here in His Word God promises
    To forgive us if we repent."

Then good little King Josiah called
  For everyone in the land
To join him in worshiping the Lord
  Within the temple grand.

And everyone knew—and still they say—
  "Josiah willingly
Turned to the Lord like no one else;
  A good little king was he."

DEAR PARENTS:

The people of Judah had been living under a series of sever problems from without and within. Tribute to foreign powers such as Babylon and Assyria drained off huge amounts of money. In addition, Judah's kings encouraged foreign idol worship in an effort to "show good faith" to her masters. King Manasseh even burned one of his own sons as sacrifice to the idol Asherah.

When Manasseh died, the people hoped for relief from his son, Amon. When it didn't come in two years, his own counselors slew him and crowned his eight-year-old son Josiah. The full story of Josiah's rule is in 2 Kings 22—23 and 2 Chronicles 34-35.

The point of the story, both here and in the Bible, is that Josiah was "good" because he led his people to worship the Lord as called for in the long-neglected and forgotten book rediscovered during the temple cleansing: the Book of Deuteronomy. Josiah's lasting tribute: "Before him there was no king like him, who turned to the Lord with all his heart and with all his soul and with all his might, according to all the Law of Moses; nor did any like him arise after him" (2 Kings 23:25).

THE EDITOR